What is work ethic? getting the most work done in the least amount of time.

Having a good work ethic is so important. If you have a good work ethic, there is so much more you will be able to do than if you have a poor work ethic.

# 1
## Good Work Quality

Josh was looking for a job. He put in an application for a job as a cashier.

Sarah also put in an application for the same job. Many people had put in their applications for the job, but only one would be hired.

The manager of the store, Mr. Smythe, interviewed each person. He found out that Josh was a hard worker and an efficient worker. He also found out that Sarah had applied for this job because she had been fired from her last one. One well-placed phone call told him that she had been fired because of laziness, and he could tell that Sarah only wanted the job for the paycheck. Who do you think Mr. Smythe would be more likely to hire?

If you show that you care about doing good work, there will be so many more opportunities for you. Some good ways you can show you want to do good quality work are:
1. Go the extra mile to do a good job
2. Work quickly, don't dawdle; but don't try to go so fast that you do poor work either.

# 2
## Doing Your Best

Megan had a job washing dishes in a restaurant. Usually she had to work late, and she was always the last one in the kitchen after the rest of the staff went home.

One Tuesday night, Megan's friend, Tammy, was having some friends over, and she invited Megan. Megan was to be at Tammy's house at 9:00.

That night things were really busy at the restaurant, and there was a lot of clean-up. Megan took one look at the messy kitchen and knew right away there was no way she could be at Tammy's by 9... That is, unless, she could get everything done really fast.

So Megan washed all the dishes as fast as she could. To save time, she swept everything that was on the floor into a corner, and completely "forgot" to wipe down the counters and stoves.

She did the rest of the work as fast as she could, then looked up at the clock. She had five minutes to get to Tammy's. If she left now, she would be only a few minutes late!

As Megan grabbed her jacket and headed for the back door, she saw that she had not put away all of the pans - she had missed a few in her hurry. She hesitated. She knew she should put them away, but if she did, she would not have time to get to Tammy's.

She stood there for a moment, gazing at the pans, and then she whirled around and hurried towards the door. It's ok, she thought. I'll just come in early tomorrow and put them away. I'm the only one here now, and I'll be the only one here then. Nobody will know.

Megan half-ran to the back door, flicked off the lights, yanked open the door... and almost bumped right into Mrs. Simpson. Megan's boss.

"Why, hello, Megan," said Mrs. Simpson softly. "May I ask where you're going in such a hurry?"

Megan started to stutter. She couldn't even begin to explain to Mrs. Simpson.

"Before you dash off, what do you say we take a look at how you're doing, hmm?"

Megan slowly found her voice. "Mrs. Simpson, is it all right we look another time? You see, my friend has invited me over to her house, and I've finished the kitchen..." she trailed off. Cold dread filled her like ice as she realized that if Mrs. Simpson saw the kind of job Megan had done, she might not have a job at all tomorrow.

Ten minutes later, Megan was washing dishes again. She had gone so fast the first time that none of the dishes were clean; they still had bits of food stuck to them. The counters had sauce spilled all over them from a chef accident, and the pile of dirt in the corner was bigger and more noticeable then Megan had realized. And then there were the pans that she had almost but decided not to put away.

So Megan had to clean the whole kitchen all over again, this time under Mrs. Simpson's supervision. She would not be fired, to her relief, but she would be docked that whole day's pay. And now, having to do everything over again, by the time she had finished, Tammy's party would have been long over.

You should always do your best no matter what you are doing. Even if you don't get caught, you will feel better knowing you did the best that you possibly could.

Instead of rushing through your work, take a little extra time to make sure you have done a good job. It may save you a lot of time in the long run!

3
Having a Cheerful Attitude

Rob and Georgia were cousins. They both worked as waiter and waitress at a diner.

Georgia always tried to be polite and have a nice attitude with the people that she served. Rob tried to be polite to the people he was serving, especially when the boss was watching.

One afternoon, an old, unpleasant-looking man walked into the diner. Rob saw him first and deliberately pretended he didn't see the old man, busying himself asking a lady who had an almost-full glass if she needed more soda.

Georgia had been in the back to get something, and she came out and saw the man. "Good afternoon, sir," she said. "Let me get you a table and I will be right with you."

The old man turned to her and said, "Well, hurry it up a bit, could you, girl?" How rude, Georgia thought, but she just smiled and said,

"Yes, sir, right away."

After he had been seated, the old man was just as unpleasant as before.

"What can I get you to drink?" asked Georgia.

The old man muttered something so quietly that Georgia couldn't hear what he said.

"I'm sorry, I didn't catch that." He mumbled a little louder, but no clearer. "Could you repeat that one more time?" Georgia said quietly, trying to be polite even though she was getting frustrated.

"I said water, girl! Are you deaf?! Water!" The old man practically shouted. A few people turned to stare.

Georgia turned red. "Yes, sir. I'm sorry. I'll be right back with your water."

The rest of the time the man was there, all he did was gave Georgia a hard time. The bread was stale (although it was fresh from the oven). Georgia was too slow. He even said this was not the meal he ordered, even though Georgia was positive that was what he said.

Georgia tried her hardest to be polite and friendly. She thought to herself, I don't know what he has been through. Perhaps he has just lost a family member, or maybe he has a mental illness and can't help being this way.

Then when he finally left, he paid for his meal and left no tip.

The next day, Georgia woke up with symptoms of the flu. She called in sick.

That afternoon, at the same time as yesterday, the rude old man came back to the diner. Rob had seen the way the man had treated Georgia the day before, and he did not want anything to do with that man.

It was a small diner, so Rob and Georgia were the only waiter and waitress at that time of day; and with Georgia sick, Rob was the only one there. So he had to deal with the old man.

He waited as long as he could before going over to the man to get him a seat. After he had sat down, the old man said, "No, no, I don't want to sit here. I want a seat away from the window.

That day was not a busy day at the diner. The old man was the only person there at the time, so there was no one at the front desk. There was no one watching, Rob was alone with the old man. "Why didn't you say so before I sat you down?"

The man just glared at Rob and said, "I said I want to sit away from the window.

So Rob moved the old man to another table. "What do you want to drink?"

The man did the same thing as the day before. He

mumbled so low Rob had to ask him to speak up. The man mumbled again.

"I can't hear you. If you want me to get you a drink, you'll have to talk louder."

"I want water, boy! I want water!" the man shouted again.

"Well, you don't have to yell," said Rob, losing his temper. "I just wanted you to talk louder!" and with that he turned and walked towards the kitchen, taking as long as he could to get the water. Then he forgot the lemon wedge on purpose and served the man cold food; and every time the man was rude, Rob was just as rude back, and when the man left without leaving a tip again, that was the last straw. Rob got so mad he was about to yell at the man, but just in time a family came into the diner, and Rob didn't want to risk his job yelling in front of them.

There was a lull in business after the family left, so Rob went into the kitchen to complain about the old man to his boss, leaving out the parts about how he had been rude right back to the man. The boss just shook his head and turned away. Rob described how the old man had treated Georgia the day before, and the boss told him that Georgia had not mentioned a nasty old man.

The old man didn't come back to the diner. He was forgotten in a few days. About a week later, Rob got a letter in the mail. It was about the nasty old man he had been so rude to. The one Georgia had been polite to.

As Rob read the letter, his heart sank.

The man had been Rob's and Georgia's boss in disguise.

Part of having a good work ethic is doing your

work cheerfully. For one thing, it will make people want to be around you more. Do you want to have to deal with a sourpuss? Well, neither do other people!

Also, if you have a cheerful attitude, you will probably get more work done, and better quality work too. I know that when I get in a bad mood, I do not do as good quality work. I just do things carelessly!

Here's a tip to help you have a good attitude: if you act like you are in a good mood, your mood will change into a good one! Even if you are feeling like there is no use even trying to be friendly, if you just give that person a smile, or hum a little tune while you are working, you will feel a lot better!

4
## Honesty is the Best Policy

Becky worked in a small, family-owned grocery store; she sold produce. It was easy for her to get a job there because her uncle owned the store.

Instead of a steady paycheck, Becky's uncle gave her a percentage of the money she made off of the produce.

Becky's uncle was very trusting of Becky. He let her count out all the money she made at the end of the day, take out her percentage, and give the rest to him.

One Wednesday, there was an unusual number of sales. Becky made a lot of money selling produce.

There was a phone that she really wanted to buy. She made enough from selling produce so that she could afford the monthly payments on the phone, she just needed to get the money for the phone itself; she wanted the expensive one.

When Becky finished work that day, she was disappointed to see that the money she had earned for herself was not enough to buy the phone If only her percentage was just a little bit higher!

Then she had an idea. Her uncle was out of town for the week, and he had asked Becky's dad to take over until he got back. Before he had left, Becky had heard him telling her dad everything he needed to know about running the store, and about the employee's percentages; and she heard him say, "Don't worry about Becky; she knows how much she is allowed to take out of the sales. Now, this is how much Caroline…"

So Becky's dad didn't know just how much Becky was allowed to take out of what she made. So, if she took just a little bit more for herself, no one would know. Even if her dad did know how much she took out, he would just think that was how much she always got. It was brilliant!

Just then Jodi, Becky's cousin, came over. Being the owner's daughter, Jodi got an easy job working in frozen foods.

"Hi, Becky. Are you done?"

"Jodi, I have something to tell you. It has to be an

absolute secret, and you can be in on it, too. Can I trust you?" whispered Becky.

"Of course you can, Becky," Jodi replied. "You know you can trust me with any secret."

Becky took a deep breath. Should she really tell her cousin her plan? Or should she keep it to herself? She decided to tell Jodi.

"Jodi," she began, "I heard Uncle Scotty telling Dad how to run the store..." Becky told her cousin all about her plan. "And you can do the same thing! I listened for a little while longer, and he said that Jodi also knows what she is doing, she knows how much to take. "... So Daddy would never know! What do you think? Are you in?"

Jodi just stared, horrified. "No! I couldn't do that to Uncle George! I'm shocked that you would even think of doing something like that!"

"You're not going to tell on me, are you?" asked Becky, worried.

"No, I gave you my word that I wouldn't; but, Becky, you mustn't!"

Becky didn't listen. She was too excited about her idea to throw it away just because Jodi wouldn't join her. So she pretended to agree with Jodi.

"You're right," she said, "it just wouldn't be right. I'm sorry I suggested it, Jodi. I'll see you tomorrow morning."

And with that Becky went into the back room to count out her 'fair percentage'.

Jodi, however, wasn't so easily convinced. I know she was lying, Jodi thought. There's no way she got that idea out of her head so easily. I know the right thing to do would be to tell Uncle George that Becky took more money, but I gave her my word I wouldn't tell! Oh, what do I do?

In the back room, Becky took every precaution she could think of to avoid getting caught. She even carefully counted how much she did take and used a calculator to see what percent she took, so if her dad asked her what her percentage was she could give him an answer that matched what she had taken. She congratulated herself on her brilliance.

The next day, when Scotty arrived back home, he called George and asked him if it was all right to take Becky out for an ice cream cone. George said sure.

After Scotty paid for the ice cream, he and Becky went for a walk in the park while they ate their cones.

"So, how did things go at the store while I was gone?" Scotty asked.

"Fine," said Becky. "We had a really busy day, but not much else. Usual business. Must have been a small holiday I didn't know about." Becky remembered in the back of her mind what she had done in the back room. Had Jodi told on her?

"Do you like that job you have?" asked Uncle Scotty.

"Yes, very much. I want to thank you for giving it to me."

Scotty laughed. "You're welcome, for the thousandth time. What about the pay?"

Now Becky was sure Jodi had told on her. "Fine, Uncle Scotty. I have saved enough for that phone now."

"Good for you." He paused. "Look, Becky, there's something I wanted to talk to you about."

Becky had to stop herself from gasping. This was it! She had been discovered! She would never speak to that rat Jodi again for the rest of her life.

She looked up at her uncle. "What is it, Uncle Scotty?"

"How much did you make yesterday? Do you still have it with you?" Scotty knew that Becky always put her share of the money right into a little white sack her Aunt Penny had made for her.

"Yes, I do. It's still in my purse. I never did have the time to take it out last night."

"Can I see it, please?" he asked. Becky gulped. She slowly took the sack out of her purse and handed it to her uncle. He opened it and counted the money carefully, then looked at Becky. "Wow," he said, "that must have been a really good day for you to make this much.

"Look, Becky, what I wanted to talk to you about is this; I know you would never cheat me, right? I trust you to take your percentage of the money."

"Of course, Uncle Scotty. I would never take more than I was supposed to. You told me how much to take, and I appreciate that amount."

This is it, Becky thought in a panic. Jodi broke her promise to me and told him.

Becky decided to play innocent. It would be her word against Jodi's, and she would have to be proven guilty. Besides, in the rush of the moment she had told Scotty a lie. Now it was too late to turn back and tell him the truth. Becky would have to stick to her story.

"Becky, I wanted to tell you that I'm going to buy that phone for you, because you're such a great employee. That money you made yesterday; put it into your savings. Is that ok?"

Becky was stunned. This was not what she had expected. She knew that letting her uncle buy the phone would be absolutely crossing the line after what she did. There was no way her conscience would allow her to do that.

On the other hand, she also knew that if she told him what she'd done, he would know she had stolen and lied.

Becky felt miserable. What she had thought of as a harmless little bonus, she now wished she had never done. She had to make a decision, fast!

"Uncle Scotty, there's something I need to tell you."

Becky told him in detail what she had done the day before, and finished with, "I know it was wrong. I'm sorry, Uncle Scotty."

Her uncle was silent for what seemed like an eternity. Finally he turned to her and said, "Becky, I'm disappointed that you would do something like that, and then lie about it; but I also want you to know that I'm proud of you for telling me. I know how hard that had to have been for you. I'll have to ask you to put back the extra money that you took, but you still have your job; and because you did the right thing in telling me, I'm still going to buy you the phone."

Becky couldn't believe it. Her uncle wasn't angry with her, and she still had her job!

"Becky, do you want to know a secret?" Scotty asked. Becky nodded.

"I already knew you had taken the extra money, even before you told me."

Again, Jodi popped into Becky's head. So she really had told on her! Becky promised herself she would never speak to her cousin again.

"Jodi…" she started, and then stopped.

"Jodi?" said Scotty, puzzled. "I haven't seen her since I got back. She's been over at a friend's house all day. I came straight to your place after talking to Aunt Penny."

"Then how…"

"There's a security camera in the back room," he said with a sly grin, "to keep people from breaking in and stealing money."

No matter what, you should always be honest with people. If you get a bad reputation for telling lies, it will be very hard for anyone to believe anything you say, even when you do tell the truth! If you are always truthful, your word will be valuable. If not, your word is worthless.

## 5
### There's no "I" in "Team"

Sam had heard that saying many times. There's no "I" in "Team".

Sam was on the school's basketball team. He always agreed that teamwork was one of the most important things to have in a team, perhaps just as important as the individual players having skill. And on the court he lived by this. Sam was definitely a team player.

If one of his teammates was trapped with the ball, Sam was right there to help. If Sam found himself unable to make shot, he didn't try to break his way through, but passed the ball to someone else.

At work, though, it was a different story.

Sam worked part-time as a mechanic. He worked after school and on Saturdays.

At work, Sam always wanted to do things his own way. If he thought one of his fellow mechanics wasn't doing something right, he would come over and tell him so, and then take his friend's tools and show him the 'right' way to do it, which was whatever way Sam thought was the way to do it.

At first it was nice, everyone thought of Sam as a helpful, caring person, who really knew what he was doing. Then, after a while, it began to get annoying. Sam began correcting every little thing the other mechanics were trying to do. They were all doing good quality work, but if they weren't doing it the way Sam had showed them to, he would get angry.

Once, Sam was replacing a tire on a truck, and another mechanic, Stanley, was replacing a car's battery. Stanley's customer was watching through the glass window that divided the waiting room from the mechanics. Suddenly, Sam stood up and went over to Stanley.

"Stanley," he said, "you're doing it wrong. Here, you need to do it like this; it will save you a lot of time, and you won't risk damaging these cords, and…"

Stanley looked over at his customer in embarrassment. Sam was making him look so stupid! With Sam telling him what to do, he must have looked like some untrained new mechanic who had to be told what to do by another. No one wanted that kind of person working on her car!!

And it didn't stop there. Soon, Sam even started telling mechanics who had been in the shop longer than he had what to do; before long, Sam was desperately trying to get all the customers he could, working on several different cars at a time.

In that shop, the mechanics had always taken turns with the cars, so everyone got a fair chance for pay - they got a percentage of what the customer paid, instead of an hourly pay; but whenever Sam saw a customer come into the shop, he hurried into the waiting room before anyone else could get there and told the person he would be their mechanic.

All of the other mechanics were getting annoyed with Sam. When they saw him coming, they groaned quietly, and they talked about him behind his back.

No one wanted to confront him, though. As rude as he was, he was a wonderful mechanic and was making the shop a lot of money; no one wanted to risk angering him and causing him to quit.

One Monday, the boss had hired a girl named Cassandra. She was to work after school and on Saturdays.

This was a strictly equal-opportunity mechanic shop; no one made fun of her for being a girl mechanic - besides, they could tell she had a lot of experience.

When Sam came in and saw Cassandra working on an engine, he hurried over to her.

"New girl, huh?" he said loudly. "Here, let me show you how to do this. Now, you have to be really careful, or… Here, let me show you." Sam took Cassandra's tools and started to work on the engine; then he ended up finishing the whole thing himself.

Cassandra tried to tell him that she appreciated his help, but was perfectly capable of doing it herself. Every time she tried to tell him she knew how to do it, he interrupted her and told her to just sit down and watch. Finally she gave up trying and just sat there and watched him work.

It was the same story for every vehicle Cassandra tried to work on. Sam would always come over and show her the 'proper' way to do it.

After about a week, Cassandra was getting really tired of it. During the lunch break, the other mechanics joked with her, saying that with Sam helping her so much, at least he left them alone most of the time.

"Why don't you tell him he is being rude?" she asked. "You have all been here a lot longer than I have; surely you are so sick of it you're willing to do something about it?"

Bobby looked at her and said, "We would, but, you see, he makes the company a lot of money. The blowhard is as good as he tells everyone he is. We don't want to lose him by making him mad."

"Well, gosh, somebody needs to. I don't want to, because I've only been here a week, and I don't want to sound like some new girl who came in and started bossing Sam around; but if nobody else is going to say anything to him, I will."

Nobody said a word. All three of them just stared at Cassandra.

After a few moments of silence, Stanley said quietly, "Cassandra, I think you may have yourself a challenge."

George nodded. "All kidding aside, no one even

wants to be around Sam any more."

Cassandra decided she would have to do it. It would be best for Sam, she told herself. He would have a lot more friends if he weren't bossy.

Sam had to leave early that day. So Cassandra wouldn't be able to talk to him until the next day after school. With Sam being gone, Cassandra worked her heart out, so happy to not have anyone telling her she was doing it wrong.

The next afternoon, when Cassandra arrived, Sam was already there. She looked around and realized with a shock that everyone had stopped their work and was staring at her. Stanley gave her a thumbs-up.

She took a deep breath and slowly walked over to Sam.

"Hi, Cassie," he said cheerfully. "What's up?"

"Sam, I need to talk to you, if you have a minute."

Out of the corner of her eye, she spotted George. He was staring straight at her, hanging on her every word. She was sure Bobby and Stanley were staring, too, wondering what she would say to Sam.

"Alone," she finished. There was no way she would tell him with everyone listening!

"Sure, Cassie. Be right with you." He slammed the hood down, and led Cassandra to the waiting room. "There's no one in there now," he said. "The customer left on an errand with her friend's car."

They sat down on the carved wooden bench. "Look, Sam..." she stopped. What would be the best way to say this? Should she start by saying, 'the other mechanics and I...", or should she leave them out of it, so if Sam got angry he would only be angry at her?

She decided it might be best if Sam realized he

was bothering everyone, not just her.

"Sam; George, Bobby, Stanley, and I were talking yesterday, and we think… we think you're being a little bit… of a nuisance."

"What do you mean?" Sam asked quietly. So far, so good, Cassandra thought. At least he didn't break out yelling and screaming at me. And then she thought, get a grip of yourself. This is Sam. He doesn't get angry; he just over-does the trying to help. He's always cheerful.

"Sam, I'm just going to be point-blank honest with you. When we're working, we know what we're doing. We really appreciate that you're trying to help us, but you're overdoing it a little bit. We're capable of doing the work by ourselves; and, well, it sort of bothers us when you keep coming up to us over and over and telling us we're not doing it right. It makes us feel like we're not good enough, so we need someone to show us how to do everything. We know you're not trying to take over, but that's what it seems like to us when you do that."

Sam had been staring down at the ground. Now he slowly looked up until his eyes met Cassandra's.

"Gosh, Cassie. I'm sorry. I really didn't mean to be bossy or try to take over anything. I was just trying to help; I didn't realize I was being a *nuisance.* I'm so sorry. I'll try really hard not to do that any more."

"It's true that nobody is perfect. We do make mistakes sometimes, but we're able to take care of them by ourselves."

"I guess I made a mistake too. I never wanted to annoy anyone; I just wanted to make sure it gets done right."

Cassandra smiled. "Just because it's the way you

do something, that doesn't mean that it's the only way. But that's ok, you know you made a mistake, and that's really important."

Sam smiled too. "What can I do to make it up to you and the guys?" he asked.

"Well, I think you could go out and apologize to Stanley, Bobby, and George. I think that would mean a lot to them. After that, just try to think about it a little more when you're working, and try to correct yourself when you know you're making a mistake."

"Thanks, Cassandra. You're a true friend for telling me this. I never would have known I was being rude, and I probably would have lost the few friends I have."

"You're a really great person to be around, Sam. You just have a few flaws. Everybody does. I do, Stanley does, and everyone does. It's just the way we were made."

Sam got up and left the waiting room. He walked over to where the other mechanics were working, and cleared his throat.

"George, Bobby, Stanley, I realize I have been a real pain to be around lately. I'm really sorry for trying to take over your jobs and for telling you you're not doing it right. I never should have implied you're not good workers. Even if you did make a mistake, I know now that's not the way to say so, by telling you you're wrong and taking your tools. I'm sorry. Can you forgive me?"

In unison, they all nodded.

"Of course we can, Sam," said Bobby.

"That really means a lot to us," said George.

"We understand that you were trying to help us," said Stanley.

Sam grinned. "Then let's get to work! Today's a busy day, and those cars won't fix themselves! George, I believe it's your turn for a shot at the customer - and I promise I won't interfere!

When you can work together with other people, there are so many benefits you can have. For example, work will get done a lot faster, and people will want to be around you more. Because, like I said before, nobody wants to be around a sourpuss. Well, no one wants to be around a bossy know-it-all either! No offense if you are a bossy know-it-all... ☺

6
Get to it!

Sandy was considered a lazy worker. She worked hard when she was doing something, and she did good work, but she would never work on her own. She always put off jobs and chores until someone told her to do it.

Sandy had just turned sixteen a few days ago. She was trying to get a job, so she would have a little bit of spending money over the summer. She was having some trouble - no one wanted to hire her. They had called her references and found out she was lazy, so she had turned to walking dogs and baby-sitting.

When she was walking dogs, she would often take them to fenced-in dog park and just let them off the leash to have fun, unless she was specifically instructed to walk with them around a certain area. Why not? she thought. At the park, they get the exercise they need, and I don't even have to do anything!

It was the same thing with her baby-sitting jobs. She asked the parents on the phone to please make sure the child had already eaten dinner (because Sandy didn't want to have to cook anything), and if she did have to make dinner, she made something simple, like a sandwich or canned spaghetti-Os. There was really nothing *wrong* with making spaghetti-Os for dinner, but Sandy was a really, really good cook (when she was in the mood), capable of making something really good for the kids.

At home, Sandy slacked off with her chores. She let her room get extremely messy, and she wouldn't clean it up until her mom or dad told her too, and even then, she had a hard time staying on task and finishing cleaning. She went for as long as she could without washing the dishes; she would sneak upstairs to her room and read until her mom came up and forced her to do the dishes.

Once every two weeks, Sandy slept over at her friend Misty's house. On the weeks that Sandy didn't go to Misty's house, Misty came to hers.

Almost every time she spent the night at Misty's, she took advantage of being the guest. She didn't offer to help Misty's mother make dinner, and all she wanted to do with Misty was lay around and watch TV. The first few times she was at Misty's house, she made the bed in the morning, because she wanted to make a good impression on Misty's parents; but after a while, she just stopped altogether. She went home leaving the bed unmade. Sandy also left big messes for Misty and her parents to clean up afterwards; for example, she wanted to make cookies one night with Misty, but after the cookies were in the oven, Sandy dumped the dirty dishes into the sink and left them for Misty's mom.

Misty was just the opposite. Whenever she came over to Sandy's house, she always helped with the chores (and there were a lot of chores, because Sandy didn't help out with them hardly at all), cleaned up after herself and Sandy, and made the guest room nice and tidy before she left.

Misty's parents noticed how Sandy was beginning to get careless. They began to not want her to spend the night at their house anymore, because she always left such a big mess. So Misty had to tell Sandy that she couldn't come over to their house anymore, but Misty could still go to Sandy's house.

Sandy's parents also saw that Sandy was using her friend, getting her to do all of her chores around the house they told her that Misty was such a kind and considerate girl, and Sandy shouldn't take advantage of her like that. So, until Sandy's work habits started to improve, and she started to do chores on her own without being asked, she would not be able to have Misty over as her guest anymore.

As time went on, Misty started to resent Sandy because of her laziness. The girls no longer had sleepovers at each other's houses, even though they sometimes got their parents' permission. They still saw each other at school, but they were talking to each other less and less. Misty began to see how Sandy had used her, almost as a maid, and Sandy decided that being around Misty meant she would probably have to work somehow, and she wasn't willing to make that sacrifice for her friend.

Eventually, both girls split up and went their separate ways.

Sandy got a minimum-wage job working for a fast-food restaurant, lost the job after a few weeks, got another minimum-wage job, lost it, and just decided to stick to walking dogs.

About five years later, Sandy was flipping through her address book, and she found Misty's number in the back. She decided to give her long lost friend a call.

The two young ladies talked for about half an hour. Sandy found out that Misty had a good job, she had been there almost three years now, and between the money she and her fiancé made, they would be able to buy a nice house. Sandy replied that she had jumped around from job to job, but she had managed to keep this one for over five months so far. She was paying rent on a little apartment.

Sandy did not have a fiancé; she didn't even have a boyfriend; no one wanted to have a serious relationship with her, because she still had the same laziness that had caused her and Misty to split up.

A very important part of having good work ethics is not only working well, but working without having to be told to. Just look around, and when you see a job that needs to be done, do it! Don't say, "Hey, Mom, the laundry needs to be done". Do it yourself! It will make life a lot easier for everyone around you.

Don't just do it because you have to; do it out of love. If you mow the lawn so your Dad doesn't have to, or make dinner so your sister, even though it was her turn to make dinner, will have time to finish her school project and turn it in on time. Trust me, people will notice when you do things on your own. You may not think they notice or care, but they definitely do, and it makes all the difference in the world.

7
Leading by Example

William was almost always irritated with his little sister, Ella. Is seemed she was always doing something to annoy him! She was rude to him; she would sneak into his room and steal his things; and when he told her to do something, she would go in that direction to do it, but as soon as she knew she was out of sight, she would run and hide, then sneak into her room to play, and when William asked her if she did what he asked, she denied him ever telling her anything. Ella was just plain annoying.

One day, William just got fed up with his sister. He told her, "Look, *Bella,* if you disobey me one more time, you can bet your boots Mom will hear about it!" William knew his sister hated being called Bella.

Ella immediately stuck her tongue out at William and ran to her room. No, William thought. I can hear her footsteps. She's not going to her room. He broke into a run, racing to catch up to Ella. *She's going to mine!*

William got to his room just a moment too late. As he was racing down the hallway, he heard a tremendous crash. "Ella! Get out of there, *now!"*

As he reached his doorway, Ella shoved her way past him and took off and a run. William took a deep breath and glanced into his room, and almost had a heart attack.

The room was in shambles. In the few seconds Ella had been in there, she had wreaked havoc!

William had a huge glass trophy case his grandfather had made for him. William didn't have any trophies, so he kept unframed pictures in it. They were all over the place in there; taped to so many different places on the glass, you couldn't see through them to the other side. A wall of pictures!

Now his precious trophy case lay in a million pieces, scattered all over the floor. Pictures were scattered everywhere; some blew around the room, because William had left his window open that morning. He hurried to shut it before some of the pictures blew out.

William stared down at the broken glass. He couldn't believe it! Why would Ella do such a thing? Right then, William hated his sister so much, he felt he could have murdered her.

Stunned, William slowly walked towards his mother's bedroom. She was vacuuming the floor. He couldn't speak; he beckoned for her to follow him, and led her down the hall.

When she saw the glass, she gasped. "Oh, William, what happened?"

William suddenly found his voice. "It was that brat, Ella! I've told you and told you, she can't do anything right and she hates me! She came in and did this just for spite!"

"Now, William, that's not fair. I'm sure there are two sides to this story. Ella wouldn't just do something like this for no reason. What were you doing to her?"

William's mouth fell open. "Nothing! I wasn't doing anything to her!"

Just then, Ella ran back into the room. "No, I didn't!" she shouted. "He was threatening me!

William's mom sighed. 'William," she said, "Start cleaning up the broken glass. I'll have a talk with Ella, and later I want to have a talk with you." she left the room with Ella.

A little while later, him mom came back into his room. "I'm not going to lecture you," she said. "I know you know what you did to Ella. And I think you know it was wrong.

"William, yelling at her and ordering her around isn't the way to do things. It will only make her mad, and you don't really get the effects you want from her, do you? When she's mad at you, she isn't going to do what you say.

"I was reading a book at the library last week. It gave me some helpful hints, and I think you can use this one.

"Instead of trying to be the boss of Ella, try to be a good example for her. If you try asking her nicely to do things, I think you will have better results."

"But I just can't do that," said William. "If she's not yelled at, she doesn't pay attention. Before you yell at her to do something, first you have to yell to get her attention!"

"Will, please just trust me. Just give it a try.

"And being a good example doesn't mean just not yelling at her. I think one of the reasons she's rude to you is because you're rude to her first. You're the older one, and it's your responsibility to act more mature. If Ella sees that you're not going to be childish, she will follow your example. "

"But what about my trophy case?" asked William. "I think she should have to pay for it out of her savings."

"Don't worry about it, Will. I know what to do."

"Are you going to make her replace it?"

"No," she replied.

"No?! But Grandpa made that for me! In fact, even if she did have to buy a new one, it *couldn't* be replaced!"

"Just trust me, Will. And think about what I said. Give it a try, and you might be surprised."

Yeah, William thought. I'll be surprised that something my own mom told me doesn't work. I might as well try it, though. The way I'm doing it now doesn't seem to be working.

So William tried extra hard to be a good example to Ella. When he saw her doing something she shouldn't, he tried to gently correct her. It made him sick to think of being so nice to his bratty little sister, but he did it to make his mom happy.

Soon, he realized that he was beginning to see results. It was getting easier to ask Ella nicely to do things, and she was actually listening to him and doing what he said (most of the time)!

It had been close to the end of November when William's trophy case had been smashed. Now it was about halfway through December.

One Saturday morning, William's mom came up to him and asked him, "Well, William, how are you doing with being Ella's example? Is it working for you?"

William had his pride. He cringed at the thought of telling his mom she was right and he had been so wrong.

"Um, well, Ella's not being quite as bratty," he faltered. "In fact, she's acting almost human."

His mom laughed. "Oh, William, you exaggerate so. You don't think I have been watching and noticing. I have. She's getting better all the time. Those arguments that you used to have so often that you thought I didn't know about; I could hear every word of them. And now I don't hear nearly as many."

William grinned sheepishly. "Maybe… maybe she's just being good because she knows Santa Clause is coming to town?"

His mom laughed so hard that William started laughing too. "Right. I'm sure that's it, William. It means nothing that she stopped believing in Santa Clause four year ago."

William rolled his eyes. "Of course it means nothing. She's so forgetful; she probably forgot to not believe in him."

"Ok, all joking aside, do you think being a good example for her is helping at all?"

"Yes," replied William, "I think it really is. You're right, we're not fighting as much; and she's not being as rude to me anymore."

"Good. What about you, are you being more productive and not do rude to people?"

"Mom!" William exclaimed, "what are you insinuating?? I'm always the perfect angel!"

Again, both of them burst into fits of laughter. "I know someone who's going to get a stocking full of coal," said William, gasping to catch his breath. "And this time, it's not Ella!"

On Christmas morning, Ella woke up William and pulled him into the living room to open presents. William told her that she could open a few of hers, but he was going to wait for their mom and dad.

They tiptoed into the living room and turned on the light. William looked around, and gasped. Over by the Christmas tree, there was an absolutely *huge* wrapped present. He and Ella hurried over to it.

"William, it has your name on it," said Ella, sounding disappointed.

William decided to open just this one before his mom and dad got up.

It was a brand-new trophy case. Inside was a note that said,

'Your mom told me what happened. Hope you like this one as much as the one that broke! Love, Uncle Charley'

Many times, if someone behaves immaturely, if you set a good example, chances are they will follow your example. Don't get discouraged if they don't, though. If at first you don't succeed; try, try again!

Daniel was almost always late for everything. Not only was he usually late for work, he was late for appointments, school, and other schedules.

Whenever Daniel told his friends he would meet them at a certain time, his friends would arrive ten minutes after the set time so they wouldn't have to wait for him; and sometimes after ten minutes had passed, they still had to wait a while longer.

Occasionally, he didn't show up at all, he just left his friends waiting for him; then the next day when he saw them, he would just say, "Sorry, guys. I completely forgot."

Daniel's friends put up with his being late because they felt sure he would change. Surely, they thought, he wouldn't be this irresponsible for his whole life?

After a while, though, they began to see that Daniel was not going to change. Some of them got fed up; they told him they would meet him somewhere at a certain time, and if he wasn't there exactly on time, they just left.

One by one, all his friends got tired of his games and no longer wanted to meet him anywhere. A few of them went so far as to tell him they didn't want to hang out with him any more.

All, that is, except one.

Jacob and Daniel had been friends since first grade. They did everything together. They put up with each other's faults, knowing they each had faults of their own.

When Daniel and Jacob became friends, Daniel was never late for anything. He really cared about being on time. Over time, though, Jacob noticed that his friend was slowly changing from an always-early fanatic to an always-late… well, un-fanatic.

Finally, when it got so bad that Daniel was absolutely undependable, Jacob knew he had to do something. He was one of the few people that still wanted to meet with Daniel and actually waited for him. It looked like nobody else was going to help Daniel.

So Jacob made phone call after phone call, and finally found exactly what he was looking for. He had found a private 'tutor'; she claimed she would be able to teach Daniel to be "A punctual young man in six months or less". He told the tutor he would call her back, and then he called Daniel.

"Look, buddy, there's something I need to talk to you about." Jacob told Daniel about why he was slowly losing friends. Then he told him about the 'tutor' he had found.

"…So, are you willing to give it a try?"

Daniel was silent for a moment. Jacob thought he might have hung up. Then he said, "Ok. I'll do it. Tell her I'll be there."

The first lesson was Tuesday, right after school. Daniel was to be there twice a week, on Tuesdays and Thursdays. Jacob walked with Daniel to the first lesson, to see what the lady was like. "This is one class you'd better be on time for," he said, only half-joking.

Within the first month of the classes, Jacob could see definite improvement in Daniel's punctuality. He was on time for school most of the time, and when he met Jacob at places, he was right on time and even sometimes early.

Daniel improved rapidly. Instead of taking six

months, it took only four and a half for the teacher to declare him 'punctual'. Jacob decided to throw a surprise party. He called Daniel. "Hey, Daniel, can you meet me at my house at… oh, about six?"

"Sure, Jacob, I'll be there."

Then Jacob called all his and Daniel's friends and families. It was a Saturday, so almost everyone was available.

That evening, Jacob told everyone to find a place in the house where they would hide. Jacob would be sitting on the sofa looking casual when Daniel walked in. when he gave the signal (Daniel, guess what?), everyone would jump out and shout, "Surprise!"

5:55. "Ok, everyone," called Jacob, "Get in place! Our guest of honor will be here any minute now!"

6:00. "Any minute now."

6:10. "I'm sorry, people. He probably had to do a chore for his mom. I'm sure he'll be here soon."

6:30. People start leaving. Jacob is embarrassed and apologizing.

7:00, at Daniel's house. Daniel is in his bedroom, playing a video game. He looks up at the clock and gasps. "Oh, no! I was supposed to meet Jacob an hour ago!" He grabs his jacket and runs out the door.

7:10. Daniel knocks on Jacob's door and hurries into the house (that's the kind of friendship Jacob and Daniel have; they are always welcome to just come right into each other's houses.). The house is empty, but Daniel can tell there had been a party here - there were unopened snacks and sodas on the table, and there were balloons and a "Great Job" banner.

Daniel didn't know it at the time, but he had been

late for his own party.

Dependability as a very crucial work ethic. You don't want to be labeled as undependable, do you? If you aren't dependable, people will have a hard time trusting you when you say you will be somewhere.

Jane had seven brothers and sisters - three boys and four girls. Jane and her family lived on a ranch in Nebraska. Jane and her sisters did all the housework, and her brothers and father did all the work out on the ranch.

Her mother had died when Jane was three years old. So she and her siblings lived with their father. He made enough money with the ranch to support all of them.

From youngest to oldest, it was Justin, 10; Jane, 12; Ron, 13; Gracie and Macy, twins, 14; Adelle, 16; Margaret, 17; and Dillon, 19.

Every day, when the girls finished the housework, they were allowed to go out and ride the horses. They were allowed to ride wherever they wanted to; their father's only rules were that they couldn't ride the same horses every day, because all tem of them needed exercise, not just the girls' favorites; the girls had to be back before dark; and when they were done, the horses had to be put in their pen with the gate latched.

One Saturday afternoon, the girls finished the housework early. All there was left to do was sweep the floors.

"Jane," said Gracie, "If you'll finished sweeping the floors in a hurry, we'll saddle your horse for you and wait for you at the gate."

"Sure!" cried Jane eagerly. Being the shortest in the family, except for Justin, it was hard for her to saddle a horse.

Jane swept the floors as fast as she could, then ran

out the door.

On the way to the horse pen, she saw Dillon carrying hay to the truck. "Dillon!" she called. "Tell Daddy we're going to the horses!" Dillon flashed her thumbs-up, and she kept running.

When she reached the horse pen, she could see her sisters waiting for her by the gate, already on their horses. Macy held her own reins and the reins of a gold-and-reddish horse.

"Sunset!" cried Jane. Sunset was her favorite horse. She loved them all, of course, but she just especially loved Sunset. She climbed up onto the horse and Macy handed her the reins.

Gracie grinned. "Where shall we go today?"

"Let's let the horses decide," said her twin, laughing. "They know their way around, so why not?"

So the girls let the horses travel wherever they wanted to. Sometimes the horses walked, sometimes they ran.

After a while, they came to the lake. Actually, it was somewhere in between a tiny lake or a huge pond.

"I should have known it," said Adelle with a smile. "They love it here."

The girls got off their horses and skipped rocks while the horses got a drink. They never needed to tie the horses up; they were very tame, loving horses, and would never run away.

After a while, Margaret said, "We'd better go back, y'all. It'll be getting dark soon, and this here lake is a long way from the ranch."

So they gathered up the horses and headed back. This time, they wanted to ride like the wind. They loved riding at full speed! Jane pulled ahead on

Sunset, but Macy easily caught up and passed her; she was on Blackie, the fastest horse.

"Hey, wait up, y'all," called Adelle. "Mary's getting old; she ain't the cyclone she used to be!"

The girls arrived at the ranch just as the sun was setting. "Just look at that sunset," said Jane. "It looks like melting fire, don't it?"

Thinking Jane had mentioned his name, Sunset snorted and tossed his head.

"I think it's going to rain tonight," said Macy. "I can tell by the way the horses are acting." it was true. The horses were getting a little skittish, like they always did before a storm.

"Jane," said Margaret, "would you mind feeding the horses and giving them their water tonight?"

Jane glanced over at her sister. "Isn't that supposed to be Justin's job?"

"Well, yes, but maybe you could help him out this once?" She winked. "Besides, who knows? If I see that you're doing a good deed for your brother, I might be inspired to put away your saddle and bridle."

Jane got the message. She had as much difficulty taking the saddle *off* as she did getting it *on.*

By the time Jane had fed the horses and was bringing water up from the well, she could smell Adelle's homemade cornbread baking. She emptied the water into the horses' trough, and ran up to the house.

Jane and her siblings had Sundays off; they didn't have to work on the ranch or do housework. The girls usually got up really early so they could ride the horses before church; and once in a while, Justin, Ron, and Dillon would join them.

Today all eight of them got up to go riding. They

sneaked out of the house quietly so they wouldn't wake up their father. He did have to work on the ranch today, and he would need all the sleep he could get before church.

"The ground's wet", said Ron once they were outside.

"It's been storming all night," Jane replied. "I hope the horses didn't get spooked. They could easily jump that fence if they were spooked."

"They wouldn't have to, said Dillon grimly.

Jane looked up at him, puzzled. "What?"

"Someone left the gate unlatched last night. They wouldn't have to jump the fence; they could just run out the open gate. And it looks like that's exactly what they did."

It was true. The pen was empty.

"They wouldn't have gone far, would they?" asked Macy, panic creeping into her voice. "We don't tie them up when we go to the lake, and they never go far from us there.

"When a horse is spooked," said Dillon, "There's no telling what it'll do."

"There's Freckles," said Ron, pointing, "but all the rest are gone. Even old Mary."

Margaret shook her head. "We should go in and wake up Dad."

They all slowly walked towards the house. Jane walked especially slowly, because she knew the horses wee gone because of her. She remembered pouring the water into the trough and running up to the house, completely forgetting about latching the gate. As far as she could tell, though, no one knew - yet - that she was the one who had left the gate open.

When they had told their father that the horses

were gone, he was silent for a long time, and then he said, "Ok. Go get ready for church, all of you."

"Dad," said Justin quietly, "What are you gonna do about the horses? Are you gonna go and find them?"

"Justin, don't worry about it. Just go with your brothers and get ready for church."

When they were all ready for church, he said, "Y'all go and get in the truck. I want to talk to Justin; we'll be out in a minute."

While everyone else headed towards the truck, Jane hid and stayed behind. She wanted to ask her father something, but didn't want anyone to see she was staying behind, because they might try to stop her and bring her to the truck.

While she was hiding, she could hear her father talking to Justin in a low voice.

"Justin, it's your job to give food and water to the horses at night, right?" Justin was silent. Since Jane couldn't see him, she assumed he nodded.

"So that means you're the last one out with the horses after the girls get back, right?"

Justin suddenly got what his father was saying. "No!" he cried. "I didn't do it! I did not leave the gate open!"

"Justin," said his dad again, "I know you wouldn't do something like that on purpose, but you're really going to try to tell me that when you were the last one out there, you didn't check that the gate was locked? That is supposed to be the first thing you do when you go out there.

"Well, I know it is, but... Oh! I forgot! I couldn't have been the one; I wasn't even out there last night. My chores... they were already done!"

His dad looked sternly down at him. Great,

thought Justin grimly, realizing he might have made a mistake, Thanks to talking before I think, I have either left the gate open, letting out all of the horses, or I didn't do my evening chores and lied about it; but I didn't lie! It's the truth, my chores were done.

"Either way, Justin, I'm going to have to give you a whipping."

Jane gasped. She couldn't take it anymore. There was no way she could let Justin get punished for something she had done. She stepped into the room.

"Dad?"

Justin looked at her curiously. Was she here to help him or give her dad more evidence that Justin had left the gate open?

"Go wait in the truck, Jane. We'll be out in a few minutes."

"Dad, Justin didn't leave the gate unlatched. I did."

Her dad looked up at her. "What?"

"I said I left the gate open. Justin wasn't even out there. I gave the horses food and water so he wouldn't have to, and I forgot to lock the gate."

As she talked, she could see Justin's face lighting up. He had proof that he hadn't done it! Jane decided that whatever punishment her father would give her, seeing the look on Justin's face was worth it.

"Jane, Justin, both of you get in the truck or we'll be late for church. Jane, I'll decide your punishment later."

The others had been standing by the truck waiting. When they saw Jane and Justin coming, they got in.

Adelle up front; Jane on the left in the backseat; Macy in the middle; Gracie on the right; and Margaret and the boys in the bed.

On the way home, their father said, "Jane, I'm proud of you for taking responsibility for leaving the gate open, I want you to know that. But now we're minus nine horses - well, ten, actually, because we never did pen up Freckles even though we saw him, he could be long gone by now - and I can't let that go unpunished. I want you to give all the animals their food and water for a week."

"Ok, Dad," said Jane quietly. She didn't mind the extra work, though, thinking of how she had saved Justin from being unfairly punished.

As they were driving down the long, dirt driveway that led to the ranch, Jane heard a tapping on the back window. She twisted around in her seat.

It was Ron. He was tapping on the window to get their attention and pointing toward the ranch.

All ten horses were slowly walking randomly around the ranch, grazing. A few were in the open pen, drinking water, and the rest were all in plain sight.

All of them, were there.

Even old Mary.


Taking responsibility for your actions is a valuable asset. Let's say someone messes up at work and doesn't want to admit it, because he fears the boss will be mad at him. Well, nobody else did it, so it's not very likely that they're going to say that they did it. With everyone denying doing it, the boss doesn't know who to believe, and that's not really fair. It would be a lot easier if the person who made the mistake to just take responsibility and 'fess up.

I hope you enjoyed reading this book as much as I enjoyed writing it. I also hope it was really helpful to you.

If you have any questions or anything, don't hesitate to contact me. My email is eapgoose@hotmail.com. I would love to hear from you! ☺

Made in the USA
Columbia, SC
08 June 2025

59083218R00029